The Poems and Verses of
Charles Dickens

The Poems and Verses of
Charles Dickens

Collected and Edited, with
Bibliographical Notes, by

F. G. Kitton

Harper & Brothers Publishers
New York and London
1903

To
Miss Georgina Hogarth
this little volume is
respectfully dedicated

Contents

Contents

Contents

Contents

Contents

Songs, Choruses

And Concerted Pieces From

"The Village Coquettes"

A Comic Opera

1836

The Village Coquettes

ABOUT the year 1834, when the earliest of the *Sketches by Boz* were appearing in print, a young composer named John Hullah set to music a portion of an opera called "The Gondolier," which he thought might prove successful on the stage. Twelve months later Hullah became acquainted with Charles Dickens, whose name was then unknown to those outside his own immediate circle, and it occurred to him that he and "Boz" might combine their forces by converting "The Gondolier" into a popular play. Dickens, who always entertained a passion for the theatre, entered into the project at once,

3

and informed Hullah that he had a little un-
published story by him which he thought would
dramatize well—even better than "The Gon-
dolier" notion; confessing that he would rather
deal with familiar English scenes than with the
unfamiliar Venetian environment of the play
favored by Hullah. The title of "The Gon-
dolier" was consequently abandoned, and a
novel subject found and put forward as "The
Village Coquettes," a comic opera of which
songs, duets, and concerted pieces were to form
constituent parts. Dickens, of course, became
responsible for the libretto and Hullah for the
music; and when completed the little play was
offered to, and accepted by, Braham, the lessee
of the St. James's Theatre, who expressed an
earnest desire to be the first to introduce "Boz"

4

to the public as a dramatic writer. A favorite comedian of that day, John Pritt Harley, after reading the words of the opera prior to its representation, declared it was "a sure card," and felt so confident of its success that he offered to wager ten pounds that it would run fifty nights!—an assurance which at once decided Braham to produce it.

"The Village Coquettes," described on the title-page of the printed copies as "A Comic Opera, in Two Acts," was played for the first time on December 6, 1836, with Braham and Harley in the cast. In his preface to the play (published contemporaneously by Richard Bentley, and dedicated to Harley) Dickens explained that "the libretto of an opera must be, to a certain extent, a mere vehicle for the music," and that "it is scarcely fair or reasonable to judge it by those strict rules of criticism which would be justly applicable to a five-act tragedy or a finished comedy." There is no doubt that the merits of the play were based upon the songs set to Hullah's music rather than upon the play itself, and it is said that Harley's reputation as a vocalist was established by his able rendering of them.

"The Village Coquettes" enjoyed a run of nineteen nights in London during the season, and was then transferred to Edinburgh, where it was performed under the management of Mr. Ramsay, a friend of Sir Walter Scott. Sala, as a boy of ten, witnessed its first representation in London, and ever retained a vivid impression of the event; while especial interest appertains to the fact that a copy of the play became the means of first bringing Dickens into personal communication with John Forster, his life-long friend and biographer. It is more than probable that "Boz" felt a little elated by the reception accorded by the public to the "dramatic bantling," but as time progressed he realized that the somewhat unfavorable comments of the critics were not entirely devoid of truth. Indeed, when in 1843 it was proposed to revive the play, he expressed a hope that it might be allowed "to sink into its native obscurity." "I did it," he explained, "in a fit of damnable good-nature long ago, for Hullah, who wrote some very pretty music to it. I just put down for everybody what everybody at the St. James's Theatre wanted to say and do, and

7

what they could say and do best, and I have
been most sincerely repentant ever since." The
novelist confessed that both the operetta and a
little farce called "The Strange Gentleman"
(the latter written as "a practical joke" for
the St. James's Theatre about the same time)
were done "without the least consideration or
regard to reputation"; he also declared that he
"wouldn't repeat them for a thousand pounds
apiece," and devoutly wished these early dra-
matic efforts to be forgotten. Apropos of this,
the late Frederick Locker-Lampson has recorded
that when he asked Dickens (about a year be-
fore the great writer's death) whether he possess-
ed a copy of "The Village Coquettes," his reply
was, "No; and if I knew it was in my house,
and if I could not get rid of it in any other way,

8

I would burn the wing of the house where it was!"

Although, perhaps, not of a high order of merit, "The Village Coquettes" is not without bibliographical interest, and may be regarded as a musical and literary curiosity. Copies of the first edition of the little play are now seldom met with, and whenever a perfect impression comes into the market it commands a good price, even as much as ten or twelve pounds—indeed, a particularly fine copy was sold at Sotheby's in 1889 for twenty-five pounds. In 1878 the words of the opera were reprinted in facsimile by Richard Bentley, for which a frontispiece was etched by F. W. Pailthorpe a year later.

The Village Coquettes

Round

HAIL to the merry autumn days,
    when yellow cornfields shine,
Far brighter than the costly cup
that holds the monarch's wine!
Hail to the merry harvest time, the gayest
    of the year,
The time of rich and bounteous crops, rejoic-
    ing, and good cheer!

'Tis pleasant on a fine spring morn to see the
buds expand,

'Tis pleasant in the summer time to view the
teeming land;

'Tis pleasant on a winter's night to crouch
around the blaze—

But what are joys like these, my boys, to
autumn's merry days!

Then hail to merry autumn days, when yellow
cornfields shine,

Far brighter than the costly cup that holds
the monarch's wine!

And hail to merry harvest time, the gayest
  of the year,

The time of rich and bounteous crops, rejoic-
  ing, and good cheer!

Lucy's Song

Love is not a feeling to pass away,

Like the balmy breath of a summer day;

It is not—it cannot be—laid aside;

It is not a thing to forget or hide.

It clings to the heart, ah, woe is me!

As the ivy clings to the old oak-tree.

13

Love is not a passion of earthly mould,

As a thirst for honor, or fame, or gold:

For when all these wishes have died away,

The deep, strong love of a brighter day,

Though nourished in secret, consumes the more,

As the slow rust eats to the iron's core.

Squire Norton's Song

That very wise head, old Æsop, said,

  The bow should be sometimes loose;

Keep it tight forever, the string you sever:—

  Let's turn his old moral to use.

The Village Coquettes

The world forget, and let us yet,

 The glass our spirits buoying,

Revel to-night in those moments bright

 Which make life worth enjoying.

The cares of the day, old moralists say,

 Are quite enough to perplex one;

Then drive to-day's sorrow away till to-

 morrow,

 And then put it off till the next one.

   Chorus—The cares of the day, etc.

Some plodding old crones—the heartless drones!

 Appeal to my cool reflection,

And ask me whether such nights can ever

   Charm sober recollection.

Yes, yes! I cry, I'll grieve and die,

   When those I love forsake me;

But while friends so dear surround me here,

   Let Care, if he can, o'ertake me.

        Chorus—The cares of the day, etc.

George Edmunds's Song

Autumn leaves, autumn leaves, lie strewn

   around me here;

Autumn leaves, autumn leaves, how sad, how

   cold, how drear!

How like the hopes of childhood's day,

Thick clust'ring on the bough!

How like those hopes in their decay—

How faded are they now!

Autumn leaves, autumn leaves, lie strewn

around me here;

Autumn leaves, autumn leaves, how sad, how

cold, how drear!

Wither'd leaves, wither'd leaves, that fly be-

fore the gale:

Withered leaves, withered leaves, ye tell a

mournful tale,

Of love once true, and friends once kind,

And happy moments fled:

Dispersed by every breath of wind,

Forgotten, changed, or dead!

Autumn leaves, autumn leaves, lie strewn

around me here!

Autumn leaves, autumn leaves, how sad, how

cold, how drear!

Rose's Song

Some folks who have grown old and sour,

Say love does nothing but annoy.

The fact is, they have had their hour,

So envy what they can't enjoy.

I like the glance—I like the sigh—

That does of ardent passion tell!

If some folks were as young as I,

I'm sure they'd like it quite as well.

Old maiden aunts so hate the men,

So well know how wives are harried,

It makes them sad—not jealous—when

They see their poor, dear nieces married.

All men are fair and false, they know,

And with deep sighs they assail 'em;

It's so long since they tried men, though,

I rather think their mem'ries fail 'em.

Duet (*Flam and Rose*)

Flam. 'Tis true I'm caressed by the witty,

The envy of all the fine beaux,

The pet of the court and the city,

But still, I'm the lover of Rose.

Rose. Country sweethearts, oh, how I despise!

And oh! how delighted I am

To think that I shine in the eyes

Of the elegant—sweet—Mr. Flam.

20

Flam. Allow me [*offers to kiss her*].

Rose. Pray don't be so bold, sir [*kisses her*].

Flam.   What sweets on that honey'd lip hang!

Rose. Your presumption, I know, I should

      scold, sir,

        But I really *can't* scold Mr. Flam.

Both. Then let us be happy together,

        Content with the world as it goes,

      An unchangeable couple forever,

        Mr. Flam and his beautiful Rose.

Squire Norton's Song

The child and the old man sat alone

   In the quiet, peaceful shade

Of the old green boughs, that had richly grown

   In the deep, thick forest glade.

It was a soft and pleasant sound,

   That rustling of the oak;

And the gentle breeze played lightly round,

   As thus the fair boy spoke:—

"Dear father, what can honor be,

   Of which I hear men rave?

Field, cell and cloister, land and sea,

    The tempest and the grave:—

It lives in all, 'tis sought in each,

    'Tis never heard or seen:

Now tell me, father, I beseech,

    What can this honor mean?"

"It is a name—a name, my child—

    It lived in other days,

When men were rude, their passions

    wild,

    Their sport, thick battle-frays.

23

When, in armor bright, the warrior bold

   Knelt to his lady's eyes:

Beneath the abbey pavement old

   That warrior's dust now lies.

"The iron hearts of that old day

   Have mouldered in the grave;

And chivalry has passed away,

   With knights so true and brave;

The honor, which to them was life,

   Throbs in no bosom now;

It only gilds the gambler's strife,

   Or decks the worthless vow."

Duet (*The Squire and Lucy*)

Squire. In rich and lofty station shine,

Before his jealous eyes;

In golden splendor, lady mine,

This peasant youth despise.

Lucy [apart; *the Squire regarding her attentively*].

Oh! it would be revenge indeed,

With scorn his glance to meet.

I, I, his humble pleading heed!

I'd spurn him from my feet.

Squire. With love and rage her bosom's torn,

And rash the choice will be;

25

Lucy. With love and rage my bosom's torn,

And rash the choice will be.

Squire. From hence she quickly must be borne,

Her home, her home, she'll flee.

Lucy. Oh! long shall I have cause to mourn

My home, my home, for thee!

Sestet and Chorus

Young Benson. Turn him from the farm! From

his home will you cast

The old man who has tilled it for years!

26

Ev'ry tree, ev'ry flower, is linked with the

past,

And a friend of his childhood appears.

Turn *him* from the farm! O'er its grassy

hill-side,

A gay boy he once loved to range;

His boyhood has fled, and its dear friends

are dead,

But these meadows have never known

change.

Edmunds. Oppressor, hear me!

Lucy.   On my knees I implore.

Squire. I command it, and you will obey.

Rose. Rise, dear Lucy, rise; you shall not kneel

before

The tyrant who drives us away.

Squire. Your sorrows are useless, your prayers

are in vain:

I command it, and you will begone.

I'll hear no more.

Edmunds.　　　　No, they shall not beg

again

Of a man whom I view with deep

scorn.

Flam. Do not yield.

28

Young Benson.

Squire.

Lucy. } Leave the farm !

Rose.

Edmunds.   Your pow'r I despise.

Squire. And your threats, boy, I disregard too.

Flam. Do not yield.

Young Benson.

Squire.

Lucy. } Leave the farm !

Rose.

Rose.   If he leaves it, he dies.

Edmunds. This base act, proud man, you shall rue.

29

Young Benson. Turn him from the farm! From
his home will you cast

The old man who has tilled it for years?

Ev'ry tree, ev'ry flower, is linked with the
past,

And a friend of his childhood appears!

Squire. Yes, yes, leave the farm! From his
home I will cast

The old man who has tilled it for
years;

Though each tree and flower is linked with
the past,

And a friend of his childhood appears.

30

Chorus

He has turned from his farm! From his

home he has cast

The old man who has tilled it for years;

Though each tree and flower is linked with

the past,

And a friend of his childhood appears.

Quartet

Squire. Hear me, when I swear that the farm

is your own

Through all changes Fortune may make;

The base charge of falsehood I never have

known;

This promise I never will break.

Rose ⎧Hear him, when he swears that the
and ⎨ farm is our own
Lucy. ⎩Through all changes Fortune may make.

Rose ⎧The base charge of falsehood he never
and ⎨ has known;
Lucy. ⎩This promise he never will break.

[*Enter Young Benson.*]

Young Benson. My sister here! Lucy! begone,

I command.

Squire. To your home I restore you again.

32

Young Benson. No boon I'll accept from that
treacherous hand

As the price of my fair sister's fame.

Squire. To your home!

Young Benson [*to Lucy*]. Hence away!

Lucy.   Brother dear, I obey.

Squire. I restore.

Young Benson.   Hence away!

Young Benson,
Rose, and Lucy. }   Let us leave.

Lucy. He swears it, dear brother.

Squire.   I swear it.

Young Benson.   Away!

Squire. I swear it.

Young Benson.   You swear to deceive.

Squire. Hear me, when I swear that the farm

　　is your own

　　　Through all changes Fortune may

　　　make.

Lucy⎫ Hear him, when he swears that the

and ⎬　farm is our own

Rose.⎭ Through all changes Fortune may make.

Young Benson. Hear him swear, hear him

　　swear, that the farm is our own

　　Through all changes Fortune may

　　make.

34

Squire. The base charge of falsehood I never
    have known,

This promise I never will break.

Lucy ⎧ The base charge of falsehood he never

and   ⎨   has known,

Rose. ⎩ This promise he never will break.

Young Benson. The base charge of falsehood
    he often has known,

This promise he surely will break.

Squire Norton's Song

There's a charm in spring, when ev'rything
    Is bursting from the ground ;

35

When pleasant show'rs bring forth the
   flow'rs
And all is life around.

In summer day, the fragrant hay
   Most sweetly scents the breeze;
And all is still, save murm'ring rill,
   Or sound of humming bees.

Old autumn comes;—with trusty gun
   In quest of birds we roam:
Unerring aim, we mark the game,
   And proudly bear it home.

The Village Coquettes

A winter's night has its delight,

  Well warmed to bed we go:

A winter's day, we're blithe and gay,

  Snipe-shooting in the snow.

A country life, without the strife

  And noisy din of town,

Is all I need, I take no heed

  Of splendor or renown.

And when I die, oh, let me lie

  Where trees above me wave;

Let wild plants bloom around my tomb,

  My quiet country grave!

Young Benson's Song

My fair home is no longer mine;

   From its roof-tree I'm driven away.

Alas! who will tend the old vine,

   Which I planted in infancy's day?

The garden, the beautiful flowers,

   The oak with its branches on high,

Dear friends of my happiest hours,

   Among thee I long hoped to die.

The briar, the moss, and the bramble,

   Along the green paths will run wild:

The Village Coquettes

The paths where I once used to ramble,

An innocent, light-hearted child.

Duet (*The Squire and Edmunds*)

Squire. Listen, though I do not fear you,

Listen to me, ere we part.

Edmunds. List to *you!* Yes, I will hear you.

Squire. Yours alone is Lucy's heart,

I swear it, by that Heav'n above me.

Edmunds. What! can I believe my ears!

Could I hope that she still loves me!

Squire. Banish all these doubts and fears,

> If a love were e'er worth gaining,

If love were ever fond and true,

> No disguise or passion feigning,

Such is her young love for you.

Squire. Listen, though I do not fear you,

> Listen to me, ere we part.

Edmunds. List to you! yes, I will hear you,

> Mine alone is her young heart.

Lucy's Song

How beautiful at eventide
  To see the twilight shadows pale,
Steal o'er the landscape, far and wide,
  O'er stream and meadow, mound and
    dale!
How soft is Nature's calm repose
  When ev'ning skies their cool dews weep:
The gentlest wind more gently blows,
  As if to soothe her in her sleep!

          The gay morn breaks,

          Mists roll away,

All Nature awakes

To glorious day.

In my breast alone

Dark shadows remain ;

The peace it has known

It can never regain.

Chorus

Join the dance, with step as light

As ev'ry heart should be to-night ;

Music, shake the lofty dome,

In honor of our Harvest Home.

The Village Coquettes

Join the dance, and banish care,

All are young, and gay, and fair;

Even age has youthful grown,

In honor of our Harvest Home.

Join the dance, bright faces beam,

Sweet lips smile, and dark eyes gleam;

All these charms have hither come,

In honor of our Harvest Home.

Join the dance, with step as light,

As ev'ry heart should be to-night;

Music shake the lofty dome

In honor of our Harvest Home.

43

Quintet

No light bound

Of stag or timid hare,

O'er the ground

Where startled herds repair,

Do we prize

So high, or hold so dear,

As the eyes

That light our pleasures here.

No cool breeze

That gently plays by night,

The Village Coquettes

O'er calm seas,

Whose waters glisten bright ;

No soft moan

That sighs across the lea,

Harvest Home,

Is half so sweet as thee!

Lyric from

"The Lamplighter"

A Farce

1838

The Lamplighter

IN 1838 Dickens agreed to prepare a little play for Macready, the famous actor, then the manager of Drury Lane Theatre. It was called "The Lamplighter," and when completed the author read aloud the "unfortunate little farce" (as he subsequently termed it) in the green-room of the theatre. Although the play went through rehearsal, it was never presented before an audience, for the actors would not agree about it, and, at Macready's suggestion, Dickens consented to withdraw it, declaring that he had "no other feeling of disappointment connected with this matter" but that which arose from the failure in attempting to serve his friend. The manuscript of the play, not in Dickens's handwriting, reposes in the Forster Library at the Victoria and Albert Museum, and in 1879 it was printed for the first time, in the form of a pamphlet, of which only two hundred and fifty copies were issued.

When rejected by Macready as unsuitable for stage presentation, "The Lamplighter" was adapted by Dickens to another purpose—that is to say, he converted it into a tale called "The Lamplighter's Story," for publication in "The Pic-Nic Papers," issued in 1841 for the benefit of the widow of Macrone, Dickens's first publisher, who died in great poverty. Between the farce and the story there are but slight differences. The duet of two verses, sung by

The Lamplighter

Tom and Betsy to the air of "The Young May-moon," cannot, of course, be regarded as a remarkable composition, but it served its purpose sufficiently well, and for that reason deserves recognition.

Duet from "The Lamplighter"

Air—"The Young May-moon"

Tom. There comes a new moon twelve times a year.

Betsy. And when there is none, all is dark and drear.

Tom. In which I espy—

Betsy. And so, too, do I—

Both. A resemblance to womankind very clear—

Both. There comes a new moon twelve times

a year;

And when there is none, all is dark

and drear.

Tom. In which I espy—

Betsy.   And so do I—

Both. A resemblance to womankind very clear.

Second Verse

Tom. She changes, she's fickle, she drives men

mad.

Betsy. She comes to bring light, and leaves

them sad.

54

The Lamplighter

Tom. So restless wild—

Betsy.   But so sweetly wild—

Both. That no better companion could be had.

Both. There comes a new moon twelve times

      a year;

        And when there is none, all is dark

        and drear.

Tom. In which I espy—

Betsy.   And so do I—

Both. A resemblance to womankind very clear.

Songs from
"The Pickwick Papers"
1837

The Ivy Green

THIS famous ballad of three verses, from the sixth chapter of *Pickwick*, is perhaps the most acceptable of all Dickens's poetical efforts. It was originally set to music, at Dickens's request, by his brother-in-law, Henry Burnett, a professional vocalist, who, by-the-way, was the admitted prototype of Nicholas Nickleby. Mr. Burnett sang the ballad scores of times in the presence of literary men and artists, and it proved an especial favorite with Landor. "The Ivy Green" was not written for *Pickwick*, Mr. Burnett assured me; but on its being so much admired the author said it should go into a monthly number, and it did. The most popular setting is undoubtedly that of Henry Russell, who has recorded that he received, as his fee, the magnificent sum of ten shillings! The ballad, in this form, went into many editions, and the sales must have amounted to tens of thousands.

I.—The Ivy Green

The Ivy Green

OH, a dainty plant is the Ivy green,

That creepeth o'er ruins old!

Of right choice food are his

meals, I ween,

In his cell so lone and cold.

The wall must be crumbled, the stone decayed,

To pleasure his dainty whim:

And the mouldering dust that years have made

Is a merry meal for him.

Creeping where no life is seen,

A rare old plant is the Ivy green.

Fast he stealeth on, though he wears no wings,

    And a stanch old heart has he.

How closely he twineth, how tight he clings,

    To his friend the huge Oak Tree!

And slyly he traileth along the ground,

    And his leaves he gently waves,

As he joyously hugs and crawleth round

    The rich mould of dead men's graves.

      Creeping where grim death hath been,

      A rare old plant is the Ivy green.

Whole ages have fled and their works decayed,

    And nations have scattered been;

The Ivy Green

But the stout old Ivy shall never fade,

   From its hale and hearty green.

The brave old plant, in its lonely days,

   Shall fatten upon the past:

For the stateliest building man can raise

   Is the Ivy's food at last.

     Creeping on, where time has been,

     A rare old plant is the Ivy green.

5

II.—A Christmas Carol

A Christmas Carol

THE five stanzas bearing the above title will be found in the twenty-eighth chapter of *Pickwick*, where they are introduced as the song which that hospitable old soul, Mr. Wardle, sung appropriately, "in a good, round, sturdy voice," before the Pickwickians and others assembled on Christmas Eve at Manor Farm. The "Carol," shortly after its appearance in *Pickwick*, was set to music to the air of "Old King Cole," and published in *The Book of British Song* (new edition), with an illustration drawn by "Alfred Crowquill"—*i.e.*, A. H. Forrester.

69

A Christmas Carol

I CARE not for spring; on his fickle

wing

Let the blossoms and buds be

borne:

He wooes them amain with his treacherous rain,

And he scatters them ere the morn.

An inconstant elf, he knows not himself

Nor his own changing mind an hour,

He'll smile in your face, and, with wry grimace,

He'll wither your youngest flower.

Let the summer sun to his bright home run,

    He shall never be sought by me;

When he's dimmed by a cloud I can laugh

    aloud,

    And care not how sulky he be!

For his darling child is the madness wild

    That sports in fierce fever's train;

And when love is too strong, it don't last

    long,

    As many have found to their pain.

A mild harvest night, by the tranquil light

    Of the modest and gentle moon,

A Christmas Carol

Has a far sweeter sheen, for me, I ween,

    Than the broad and unblushing noon.

But every leaf awakens my grief,

    As it lieth beneath the tree;

So let autumn air be never so fair,

    It by no means agrees with me.

But my song I troll out, for CHRISTMAS stout,

    The hearty, the true, and the bold;

A bumper I drain, and with might and main

    Give three cheers for this Christmas old!

We'll usher him in with a merry din

    That shall gladden his joyous heart,

And we'll keep him up, while there's bite
or sup,
And in fellowship good we'll part.

In his fine, honest pride, he scorns to hide
One jot of his hard-weather scars;
They're no disgrace, for there's much the same
trace
On the cheeks of our bravest tars.
Then again I sing, till the roof doth ring,
And it echoes from wall to wall—
To the stout old wight, fair welcome to-night,
As the King of the Seasons all!

III.—Gabriel Grub's Song

Gabriel Grub's Song

THE Sexton's melancholy dirge, in the twenty-ninth chapter of *Pickwick*, seems a little incongruous in a humorous work. The sentiment, however, thoroughly accords with the philosophic grave-digger's grewsome occupation. "The Story of the Goblins who Stole a Sexton" is one of several short tales (chiefly of a dismal character) introduced into *Pickwick;* they were doubtless written prior to the conception of *Pickwick,* each being probably intended for independent publication, and in a manner similar to the "Boz" Sketches. For

77

some reason these stories were not so published, and Dickens evidently saw a favorable opportunity of utilizing his unused manuscripts by inserting them in *The Pickwick Papers*.

Gabriel Grub's Song

BRAVE lodgings for one, brave
lodgings for one,
A few feet of cold earth, when life
is done;
A stone at the head, a stone at the feet,
A rich, juicy meal for the worms to eat;
Rank grass overhead, and damp clay around,
Brave lodgings for one, these, in holy ground!

79

IV.—Romance

Romance

IT will be remembered that while Sam Weller
and his coaching-friends refreshed themselves
at the little public-house opposite the Insolvent
Court in Portugal Street, Lincoln's Inn Fields,
prior to Sam joining Mr. Pickwick in the Fleet,
that faithful body-servant was persuaded to
"oblige the company" with a song. "Raly,
gentlemen," said Sam, "I'm not wery much
in the habit o' singin' vithout the instrument;
but anythin' for a quiet life, as the man said
ven he took the sitivation at the light-house."

"With this prelude, Mr. Samuel Weller burst
at once into the following wild and beautiful

legend, which, under the impression that it is not generally known, we take the liberty of quoting. We would beg to call particular attention to the monosyllable at the end of the second and fourth lines, which not only enables the singer to take breath at those points, but greatly assists the metre."—*The Pickwick Papers*, chapter xliii.

At the conclusion of the performance the mottled-faced gentleman contended that the song was "personal to the cloth," and demanded the name of the bishop's coachman, whose cowardice he regarded as a reflection upon coachmen in general. Sam replied that his name was not known, as "he hadn't got his card in his pocket"; whereupon the mottled-faced gentleman declared the statement to be

84

untrue, stoutly maintaining that the said coach-
man did *not* run away, but "died game—game
as pheasants," and he would "hear nothin'
said to the contrairey."

Even in the vernacular (observes Mr. Percy
Fitzgerald), "this master of words [Charles
Dickens] could be artistic; and it may fairly
be asserted that Mr. Weller's song to the coach-
men is superior to anything of the kind that has
appeared since." The two stanzas have been
set to music, as a humorous part-song, by Sir
Frederick Bridge, Mus. Doc., M.V.O., the or-
ganist of Westminster Abbey, who informs me
that it was written some years since, to celebrate
a festive gathering in honor of Dr. Turpin (!),
Secretary of the College of Organists. "It has
had a very great success," says Sir Frederick,

"and is sung much in the north of England at competitions of choirs. It is for men's voices. The humor of the words never fails to make a great hit, and I hope the music does no harm. 'The Bishop's Coach' is set to a bit of old plain-chant, and I introduce a fugue at the words, 'Sure as eggs is eggs.'"

Romance

I

BOLD Turpin vunce, on Hounslow Heath,

 Heath,

  His bold mare Bess bestrode—er;

Ven there he see'd the Bishop's coach

 A-comin' along the road—er.

So he gallops close to the 'orse's legs,

 And he claps his head vithin;

And the Bishop says, "Sure as eggs is eggs,

 This here's the bold Turpin!"

Chorus

And the Bishop says, "Sure as eggs is

eggs,

This here's the bold Turpin!"

II

Says Turpin, "You shall eat your words,

With a sarse of leaden bul-let";

So he puts a pistol to his mouth,

And he fires it down his gul-let.

The coachman, he not likin' the job,

Set off at a full gal-lop,

Romance

But Dick put a couple of balls in his nob,

And perwailed on him to stop.

Chorus (*sarcastically*)

But Dick put a couple of balls in his
nob,

And perwailed on him to stop.

Political Squibs from
"The Examiner"
1841

Political Squibs from "The Examiner," 1841

IN August, 1841, Dickens contributed anonymously to *The Examiner* (then edited by Forster) three political squibs, which were signed W., and were intended to help the Liberals in fighting their opponents. These squibs were entitled respectively "The Fine Old English Gentleman (to be said or sung at all Conservative Dinners)"; "The Quack Doctor's Proclamation"; and "Subjects for Painters (after Peter Pindar)." Concerning those productions, Forster says: "I doubt if he ever enjoyed anything more than

93

the power of thus taking part occasionally, unknown to outsiders, in the sharp conflict the press was waging at the time." In all probability he contributed other political rhymes to the pages of *The Examiner* as events prompted: if so, they are buried beyond easy reach of identification.

Writing to Forster at this time, Dickens said: "By Jove, how Radical I am getting! I wax stronger and stronger in the true principles every day." . . . He would (observes Forster) sometimes even talk, in moments of sudden indignation at the political outlook, "of carrying off himself and his household gods, like Coriolanus, to a world elsewhere." This was the period of the Tory interregnum, with Sir Robert Peel at the head of affairs.

I.—The Fine Old English Gentleman

The Fine Old English Gentleman

New Version

(To be said or sung at all Conservative Dinners)

'LL sing you a new ballad, and I'll
warrant it first-rate,

Of the days of that old gentleman

who had that old estate;

When they spent the public money at a bounti-

ful old rate

On ev'ry mistress, pimp, and scamp, at ev'ry

noble gate,

In the fine old English Tory times;

Soon may they come again!

The good old laws were garnished well with

gibbets, whips, and chains,

With fine old English penalties, and fine old

English pains,

With rebel heads, and seas of blood once hot

in rebel veins;

For all these things were requisite to guard the

rich old gains

Of the fine old English Tory times;

Soon may they come again!

The Fine Old English Gentleman

This brave old code, like Argus, had a hundred
watchful eyes,

And ev'ry English peasant had his good old
English spies,

To tempt his starving discontent with fine old
English lies,

Then call the good old Yeomanry to stop his
peevish cries,

In the fine old English Tory times;

Soon may they come again!

The good old times for cutting throats that
cried out in their need,

The good old times for hunting men who held

their fathers' creed,

The good old times when William Pitt, as all

good men agreed,

Came down direct from Paradise at more than

railroad speed. . . .

Oh, the fine old English Tory times;

When will they come again!

In those rare days, the press was seldom known

to snarl or bark,

But sweetly sang of men in pow'r, like any

tuneful lark;

The Fine Old English Gentleman

Grave judges, too, to all their evil deeds were

    in the dark;

And not a man in twenty score knew how to

    make his mark.

        Oh, the fine old English Tory times;

        Soon may they come again!

Those were the days for taxes, and for war's

    infernal din;

For scarcity of bread, that fine old dowagers

    might win;

For shutting men of letters up, through iron

    bars to grin,

Because they didn't think the Prince was alto-

gether thin,

In the fine old English Tory times;

Soon may they come again!

But tolerance, though slow in flight, is strong-

wing'd in the main;

That night must come on these fine days, in

course of time was plain;

The pure old spirit struggled, but its struggles

were in vain;

A nation's grip was on it, and it died in choking

pain,

The Fine Old English Gentleman

With the fine old English Tory days,

All of the olden time.

The bright old day now dawns again; the cry

runs through the land,

In England there shall be dear bread—in Ireland,

sword and brand;

And poverty and ignorance shall swell the

rich and grand,

So, rally round the rulers with the gentle iron

hand,

Of the fine old English Tory days;

Hail to the coming time!

W.

II.—The Quack Doctor's Proclamation

The Quack Doctor's Proclamation

Tune—"A Cobbler there was"

AN astonishing doctor has just come to town,

Who will do all the faculty per-
fectly brown:

He knows all diseases, their causes, and ends;

And he begs to appeal to his medical friends.

Tol de rol:

Diddle doll:

107

Tol de rol, de dol,

Diddle doll

Tol de rol doll.

He's a magnetic doctor, and knows how to

keep

The whole of a government snoring asleep

To popular clamors; till popular pins

Are stuck in their midriffs—and then he begins

Tol de rol.

He's a *clairvoyant* subject, and readily reads

His countrymen's wishes, condition, and needs,

The Quack Doctor's Proclamation

With many more fine things I can't tell in
rhyme—

And he keeps both his eyes shut the whole of
the time.

    Tol de rol.

You mustn't expect him to talk; but you'll
take

Most particular notice the doctor's awake,

Though for aught from his words or his looks
that you reap, he

Might just as well be most confoundedly sleepy.

    Tol de rol.

Homœopathy, too, he has practised for ages

(You'll find his prescriptions in Luke Hansard's

pages),

Just giving his patient when maddened by pain—

Of reform the ten-thousandth part of a grain.

Tol de rol.

He's a med'cine for Ireland, in portable papers;

The infallible cure for political vapors;

A neat label round it his 'prentices tie—

"Put your trust in the Lord, and keep this

powder dry!"

Tol de rol.

The Quack Doctor's Proclamation

He's a corn doctor also, of wonderful skill—

No cutting, no rooting-up, purging, or pill;

You're merely to take, 'stead of walking or riding,

The sweet school-boy exercise—innocent sliding.

Tol de rol.

There's no advice gratis. If high ladies send

His legitimate fee, he's their soft-spoken friend.

At the great public counter with one hand be-

hind him,

And one in his waistcoat, they're certain to

find him.

Tol de rol.

111

He has only to add he's the real Doctor Flam,

All others being purely fictitious and sham;

The house is a large one, tall, slated, and white,

With a lobby; and lights in the passage at night.

Tol de rol:

Diddle doll:

Tol de rol, de dol,

Diddle doll

Tol de rol doll.

W.

III.—Subjects for Painters

Subjects for Painters

(After Peter Pindar)

O you, Sir Martin,[1] and your co.
R.A.'s,

 I dedicate in meek, suggestive lays,

Some subjects for your academic palettes;

 Hoping, by dint of these my scanty jobs,

 To fill with novel thoughts your teeming

nobs,

As though I beat them in with wooden mallets.

[1] Sir Martin Archer Shee, P.R.A.

115

To you, Maclise, who Eve's fair daughters
paint

With Nature's hand, and want the maudlin
taint

Of the sweet Chalon school of silk and ermine :

To you, E. Landseer, who from year to year

Delight in beasts and birds, and dogs and deer,

And seldom give us any human vermin :

—To all who practise art, or make believe,

I offer subjects they may take or leave.

Great Sibthorp and his butler, in debate

(*Arcades ambo*) on affairs of state,

116

Not altogether "gone," but rather funny;

   Cursing the Whigs for leaving in the lurch

   Our d——d good, pleasant, gentlemanly

     Church,

Would make a picture—cheap at any money.

   Or Sibthorp as the Tory Sec.—at-War,

   Encouraging his mates with loud "Yhor!

     Yhor!"

From Treas'ry benches' most conspicuous end;

   Or Sib.'s mustachios curling with a smile,

   As an expectant premier without guile

Calls him his honorable and gallant friend.

Or Sibthorp travelling in foreign parts,

Through that rich portion of our Eastern
   charts

Where lies the land of popular tradition;

   And fairly worshipp'd by the true devout

   In all his comings-in and goings-out,

Because of the old Turkish superstition.

   Fame with her trumpet, blowing very
      hard,

   And making earth rich with celestial lard,

In puffing deeds done through Lord Chamber-
   lain Howe;

While some few thousand persons of small
gains,

Who give their charities without such pains,

Look up, much wondering what may be the
row.

Behind them Joseph Hume, who turns his pate

To where great Marlbro' House in princely
state

Shelters a host of lackeys, lords and pages,

And says he knows of dowagers a crowd,

Who, without trumpeting so very loud,

Would do so much, and more, for half the wages.

Limn, sirs, the highest lady in the land,

When Joseph Surface, fawning cap in
   hand,

Delivers in his list of patriot mortals;

Those gentlemen of honor, faith, and truth,

Who, foul-mouthed, spat upon her maiden
   youth,

And doglike did defile her palace portals.

Paint me the Tories, full of grief and
   woe,

Weeping (to voters) over Frost and Co.,

Their suff'ring, erring, much-enduring brothers.

And in the background don't forget to pack,

Each grinning ghastly from its bloody sack,

The heads of Thistlewood, Despard, and others.

Paint, squandering the club's election gold,

Fierce lovers of our constitution old,

Lords who're that sacred lady's greatest debtors;

And let the law, forbidding any voice

Or act of peer to influence the choice

Of English people, flourish in bright letters.

Paint that same dear old lady, ill at ease,

Weak in her second childhood, hard to please,

Unknowing what she ails or what she wishes;

121

With all her Carlton nephews at the door,

Deaf'ning both aunt and nurses with their

roar,

—Fighting already for the loaves and fishes.

Leaving these hints for you to dwell upon,

I shall presume to offer more anon.

W.

Prologue to
Westland Marston's Play
"The Patrician's Daughter"
1842

Prologue to
"The Patrician's Daughter"

"THE PATRICIAN'S DAUGHTER" was the title bestowed upon a play, in the tragic vein, by a then unknown writer, J. Westland Marston, it being his maiden effort in dramatic authorship. Dickens took great interest in the young man and indicated a desire to promote the welfare of his production by composing some introductory lines. To Macready he wrote: "The more I think of Marston's play, the more sure I feel that a prologue to the purpose would help it materially, and almost decide the fate of any

125

ticklish point on the first night. Now I have an idea (not easily explainable in writing, but told in five words) that would take the prologue out of the conventional dress of prologues, quite. Get the curtain up with a dash, and begin the play with a sledge-hammer blow. If, on consideration, you should agree with me, I will write the prologue, heartily." Happily for the author, his little tragedy was the first new play of the season, and it thus attracted greater attention. Its initial representation took place at Drury Lane Theatre, on December 10, 1842, and the fact that Dickens's dignified and vigorous lines were recited by Macready, the leading actor of his day, undoubtedly gave *prestige* to this performance; but the play, although it made a sensation for the moment, did not enjoy a long run, its motive being for some reason misunderstood. As explained by the editors of *The Letters of Charles Dickens*, it was (to a certain extent) an experiment in testing the effect of a tragedy of modern times and in modern dress, the novelist's Prologue being intended to show that there need be no incongruity between plain clothes of the nineteenth century and high tragedy.

"The Patrician's Daughter: A Tragedy in Five Acts," appeared in pamphlet form during the year prior to its being placed upon the boards. The Prologue was printed for the first time in the *Sunday Times*, December 11, 1842, and then in *The Theatrical Journal and Stranger's Guide*, December 17, 1842. By the kind permission of Miss Hogarth, the lines are here reproduced from the revised and only correct version in *The Letters of Charles Dickens.*

In the preface to the second edition of the play (1842), the author thus acknowledges his indebtedness to Dickens for the Prologue, which, however, does not appear in the book: "How shall I thank Mr. Dickens for the spontaneous kindness which has furnished me with so excellent a letter of introduction to the audience? The simplest acknowledgment is perhaps the best, since the least I might say would exceed *his* estimate of the obligation; while the most I could say would fail to express *mine.*"

Prologue to
"The Patrician's Daughter"

(Spoken by Mr. Macready)

NO tale of streaming plumes and
harness bright
Dwells on the poet's maiden harp
to-night;

No trumpet's clamor and no battle's fire

Breathes in the trembling accents of his lyre;

Enough for him, if in his lowly strain

He wakes one household echo not in vain;

Enough for him, if in his boldest word

The beating heart of MAN be dimly heard.

Its solemn music which, like strains that sigh

Through charmèd gardens, all who hearing die;

Its solemn music he does not pursue

To distant ages out of human view;

Nor listen to its wild and mournful chime

In the dead caverns on the shore of Time;

But musing with a calm and steady gaze

Before the crackling flames of living days,

He hears it whisper through the busy roar

Of what shall be and what has been before.

The Patrician's Daughter

Awake the Present! Shall no scene display

The tragic passion of the passing day?

Is it with Man, as with some meaner things,

That out of death his single purpose springs

Can his eventful life no moral teach

Until he be, for aye, beyond its reach?

Obscurely shall he suffer, act, and fade,

Dubb'd noble only by the sexton's spade?

Awake the Present! Though the steel-clad

    age

Find life alone within its storied page,

Iron is worn, at heart, by many still—

The tyrant Custom binds the serf-like will;

131

If the sharp rack, and screw, and chain be
gone,

These later days have tortures of their own;

The guiltless writhe, while Guilt is stretch'd in
sleep,

And Virtue lies, too often, dungeon deep.

Awake the Present! what the Past has sown

Be in its harvest garner'd, reap'd, and grown!

How pride breeds pride, and wrong engenders
wrong,

Read in the volume Truth has held so long,

Assured that where life's flowers freshest blow,

The sharpest thorns and keenest briars grow,

132

The Patrician's Daughter

How social usage has the pow'r to change

Good thoughts to evil; in its highest range

To cramp the noble soul, and turn to ruth

The kindling impulse of our glorious youth,

Crushing the spirit in its house of clay,

Learn from the lessons of the present day.

Not light its import and not poor its mien;

Yourselves the actors, and your homes the

scene.

A Word in Season

From "The Keepsake"

1844

A Word in Season

The Keepsake, one of the many fashionable annuals published during the early years of Queen Victoria's reign, had for its editor in 1844 the "gorgeous" Countess of Blessington, the reigning beauty who held court at Gore House, Kensington, where many political, artistic, and literary celebrities forgathered—Bulwer Lytton, Disraeli, Dickens, Ainsworth, D'Orsay, and the rest. Her ladyship, through her personal charm and natural gifts, succeeded in securing the services of eminent authors for the aristocratic publication; even Dickens could not resist her appeal, and in a letter to Forster (dated July,

137

1843) he wrote: "I have heard, as you have, from Lady Blessington, for whose behalf I have this morning penned the lines I send you herewith. But I have only done so to excuse myself, for I have not the least idea of their suiting her; and I hope she will send them back to you for *The Examiner*." Lady Blessington, however, decided to retain the thoughtful little poem, which was referred to in the London *Review* (twenty-three years later) as "a graceful and sweet apologue, reminding one of the manner of Hood." The theme of the poem, which Forster describes as "a clever and pointed parable in verse," was afterwards satirized in Chadband (*Bleak House*), and in the idea of religious conversion through the agency of "moral pocket-handkerchiefs."

A Word in Season

THEY have a superstition in the East,

    East,

    That Allah, written on a piece of

  paper,

Is better unction than can come of priest,

  Of rolling incense, and of lighted taper:

Holding, that any scrap which bears that name,

  In any characters, its front imprest on,

Shall help the finder through the purging flame,

  And give his toasted feet a place to rest on.

139

Accordingly, they make a mighty fuss

　With ev'ry wretched tract and fierce ora-

　tion,

And hoard the leaves — for they are not,

　like us,

　A highly civilized and thinking nation:

And, always stooping in the miry ways,

　To look for matter of this earthy leaven,

They seldom, in their dust-exploring days,

　Have any leisure to look up to Heaven.

So have I known a country on the earth,

　Where darkness sat upon the living waters,

140

And brutal ignorance, and toil, and dearth

    Were the hard portion of its sons and

    daughters:

And yet, where they who should have ope'd the

    door

    Of charity and light, for all men's find-

    ing,

Squabbled for words upon the altar-floor,

    And rent the Book, in struggles for the

    binding.

The gentlest man among these pious Turks,

God's living image ruthlessly defaces;

Their best high-churchman, with no faith in
　works,

　Bowstrings the Virtues in the market-places:

The Christian Pariah, whom both sects curse

　(They curse all other men, and curse each
　other),

Walks thro' the world, not very much the
　worse—

　Does all the good he can, and loves his
　brother.

Verses from

The "Daily News"
1846

Verses from
The "Daily News," 1846

THE *Daily News*, it will be remembered, was founded in January, 1846, by Charles Dickens, who officiated as its first editor. He soon sickened of the mechanical drudgery appertaining to the position, and resigned his editorial functions the following month. From January 21st to March 2d he contributed to its columns a series of "Travelling Sketches," afterwards reprinted in volume form as *Pictures from Italy*. He also availed himself of the opportunity afforded him, by his association with that newspaper, of once more taking up the cudgels against the Tories, and, as in the case of *The Examiner*, his attack was conveyed through the medium of some doggerel verses. These were entitled "The British Lion—A New Song, but an Old Story," to be sung to the tune of "The Great Sea-Snake." They bore the signature of "Catnach," the famous ballad-singer, and were printed in the *Daily News* of January 24, 1846.

Three weeks later some verses of a totally different character appeared in the columns of the *Daily News*, signed in full "Charles Dickens." One Lucy Simpkins, of Bremhill (or Bremble), a parish in Wiltshire, had just previously addressed a night meeting of the wives of agricultural laborers in that county, in support of a petition for free trade, and

146

her vigorous speech on that occasion inspired Dickens to write "The Hymn of the Wiltshire Laborers," thus offering an earnest protest against oppression. Concerning the "Hymn," a writer in a recent issue of *Christmas Bells* observes: "It breathes in every line the teaching of the Sermon on the Mount, the love of the All-Father, the redemption by His Son, and that love to God and man on which hang all the law and the prophets."

I.—The British Lion

The British Lion

A New Song, but an Old Story

Tune—"The Great Sea-Snake"

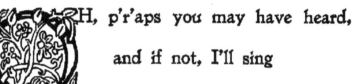H, p'r'aps you may have heard,

and if not, I'll sing

Of the British Lion free,

That was constantly a-going for to make a
spring

Upon his en-e-me;

But who, being rather groggy at the knees,

Broke down, always, before;

And generally gave a feeble wheeze

Instead of a loud roar.

Right toor rol, loor rol, fee faw fum,

The British Lion bold!

That was always a-going for to do great

things,

And was always being "sold!"

He was carried about in a carawan,

And was show'd in country parts,

And they said, "Walk up! Be in time! He

can

Eat Corn-Law Leagues like tarts!"

The British Lion

And his showmen, shouting there and then,

   To puff him didn't fail,

And they said, as they peep'd into his den,

   "Oh, don't he wag his tail!"

Now, the principal keeper of this poor old

   beast,

   Wan Humbug was his name,

Would once every day stir him up — at

   least —

   And wasn't that a game!

For he hadn't a tooth, and he hadn't a claw,

   In that "struggle" so "sublime";

And, however sharp they touch'd him on
the raw,
He couldn't come up to time.

And this, you will observe, was the reason
why
Wan Humbug, on weak grounds,
Was forced to make believe that he heard
his cry
In all unlikely sounds.
So, there wasn't a bleat from an Essex
Calf,
Or a duke, or a lordling slim;

The British Lion

But he said, with a wery triumphant laugh,

"I'm blest if that ain't him."

At length, wery bald in his mane and tail,

The British Lion growed:

He pined, and declined, and he satisfied

The last debt which he owed.

And when they came to examine the skin,

It was a wonder sore,

To find that the an-i-mal within

Was nothing but a Boar!

Right toor rol, loor rol, fee faw fum,

The British Lion bold!

155

That was always a-going for to do great

things,

And was always being "sold!"

CATNACH.

II.—The Hymn of
The Wiltshire Laborers

The Hymn of
The Wiltshire Laborers

"Don't you all think that we have a great need to Cry
to our God to put it in the hearts of our greassous Queen
and her Members of Parlerment to grant us free bread!"
                    LUCY SIMPKINS, *at Bremhill.*

God! who by Thy prophet's

hand

Didst smite the rocky brake,

Whence water came, at Thy command,

Thy people's thirst to slake;

Strike, now, upon this granite wall,

Stern, obdurate, and high;

159

And let some drops of pity fall

    For us who starve and die!

The God who took a little child

    And set him in the midst,

And promised him His mercy mild,

    As, by Thy Son, Thou didst:

Look down upon our children dear,

    So gaunt, so cold, so spare,

And let their images appear

    Where lords and gentry are!

O God! teach them to feel how we,

    When our poor infants droop,

The Wiltshire Laborers' Hymn

Are weakened in our trust in Thee,

And how our spirits stoop;

For, in Thy rest, so bright and fair,

All tears and sorrows sleep:

And their young looks, so full of care,

Would make Thine angels weep!

The God who with His finger drew

The judgment coming on,

Write, for these men, what must ensue,

Ere many years be gone!

O God! whose bow is in the sky,

Let them not brave and dare,

Until they look (too late) on high,

And see an Arrow there!

O God, remind them! In the bread

They break upon the knee,

These sacred words may yet be read,

"In memory of Me!"

O God! remind them of His sweet

Compassion for the poor,

And how He gave them Bread to eat,

And went from door to door!

CHARLES DICKENS.

New Song
Lines Addressed to Mark Lemon
1849

New Song

DICKENS, like Silas Wegg, would sometimes "drop into poetry" when writing to intimate friends, as, for example, in a letter to Maclise, the artist, which began with a parody of Byron's lines to Thomas Moore:

"My foot is in the house,
    My bath is on the sea,
And, before I take a souse,
    Here's a single note to thee."

A more remarkable instance of his propensity to indulge in parody of this kind is to be found in a letter addressed to Mark Lemon in the spring of 1849. The novelist was then enjoying a holiday with his wife and daughters at Brighton, whence he wrote to Lemon (who had been ill), pressing him to pay them a visit. After commanding him to "get a clean pocket-handkerchief ready for the close of 'Copperfield' No. 3 — 'simple and quiet, but very natural and touching' — *Evening Bore*," Dickens invites his friend in lines headed "New Song," and signed "T. Sparkler," the effusion also bearing the signatures of other members of the family party—Catherine Dickens, Annie Leech, Georgina Hogarth, Mary Dickens, Katie Dickens, and John Leech.

New Song

Tune—"Lesbia hath a Beaming Eye"

I

LEMON is a little hipped,

And this is Lemon's true posi-

tion—

He is not pale, he's not white-lipped,

Yet wants a little fresh condition.

Sweeter 'tis to gaze upon

Old ocean's rising, falling billers,

167

Than on the houses every one

That form the street called Saint Anne's

Willers!

Oh, my Lemon, round and fat,

Oh, my bright, my right, my tight 'un,

Think a little what you're at—

Don't stay at home, but come to

Brighton!

II

Lemon has a coat of frieze,

But all so seldom Lemon wears it,

New Song

That it is a prey to fleas,

    And ev'ry moth that's hungry tears it.

Oh, that coat's the coat for me,

    That braves the railway sparks and breezes,

Leaving ev'ry engine free

    To smoke it, till its owner sneezes!

        Then, my Lemon round and fat,

            L., my bright, my right, my tight 'un,

        Think a little what you're at—

            On Tuesday first, come down to

            Brighton!

                  T. SPARKLER.

Wilkie Collins's Play

"The Lighthouse"
1855

The Lighthouse

WILKIE COLLINS composed two powerful dramas
for representation at Dickens's residence, Tavis-
tock House, a portion of which had been already
adapted for private theatricals, the rooms so
converted being described in the bills as "The
Smallest Theatre in the World." The first of
these plays was called "The Lighthouse," and
the initial performance took place on June 19,
1855. Dickens not only wrote the Prologue
and "The Song of the Wreck," but signally dis-
tinguished himself by enacting the part of
Aaron Gurnock, a lighthouse-keeper, his clever

impersonation recalling Frédéric Lemaître, the only actor he ever tried to take as a model.

With regard to "The Song of the Wreck," Dickens evidently intended to bestow upon it a different title, for, in a letter addressed to Wilkie Collins during the preparation of the play, he said: "I have written a little ballad for Mary—'The Story of the Ship's Carpenter and the Little Boy, in the Shipwreck.'" The song was rendered by his eldest daughter, Mary (who assumed the rôle of Phœbe in the play); it was set to the music composed by George Linley for Miss Charlotte Young's pretty ballad, "Little Nell," of which Dickens became very fond, and which his daughter had been in the habit of singing to him constantly since her

174

childhood. Dr. A. W. Ward, Master of Peter-house, Cambridge University, refers to "The Song of the Wreck" as "a most successful effort in Cowper's manner."

I.—The Prologue

The Prologue

(Slow music all the time; unseen speaker; curtain

down.)

STORY of those rocks where doom'd ships come
To cast them wreck'd upon the steps of home,
Where solitary men, the long year through—
The wind their music and the brine their view—

Warn mariners to shun the beacon-light;

A story of those rocks is here to-night.

Eddystone Lighthouse!

(*Exterior view discovered.*)

In its ancient form,

Ere he who built it wish'd for the great storm

That shiver'd it to nothing,[1] once again

Behold outgleaming on the angry main!

---

[1] When Winstanley had brought his work to completion, he is said to have expressed himself so satisfied as to its strength, that he only wished he might be there in the fiercest storm that ever blew. His wish was gratified, and, contrary to his expectations, both he and the building were swept completely away by a furious tempest which burst along the coast in November, 1703.

The Prologue

Within it are three men; to these repair

In our frail bark of fancy, swift as air!

They are but shadows, as the rower grim

Took none but shadows in his boat with him.

So be ye shades, and, for a little space,

The real world a dream without a trace.

Return is easy. It will have ye back

Too soon to the old, beaten, dusty track;

For but one hour forget it. Billows, rise;

Blow winds, fall rain, be black, ye midnight skies;

And you who watch the light, arise! arise!

(*Exterior view rises and discovers the scene.*)

181

II.—The Song of the Wreck

The Song of the Wreck

I

THE wind blew high, the waters
raved,

A ship drove on the land,

A hundred human creatures saved

Kneel'd down upon the sand.

Threescore were drown'd, threescore were
thrown

Upon the black rocks wild,

And thus among them, left alone,

They found one helpless child.

II

A seaman rough, to shipwreck bred,

Stood out from all the rest,

And gently laid the lonely head

Upon his honest breast.

And travelling o'er the desert wide

It was a solemn joy,

To see them, ever side by side,

The sailor and the boy.

The Song of the Wreck

III

In famine, sickness, hunger, thirst,

    The two were still but one,

Until the strong man droop'd the first

    And felt his labors done.

Then to a trusty friend he spake,

    "Across the desert wide,

Oh, take this poor boy for my sake!"

    And kiss'd the child and died.

IV

Toiling along in weary plight

    Through heavy jungle, mire,

These two came later every night

    To warm them at the fire.

Until the captain said one day

    "O seaman, good and kind,

To save thyself now come away,

    And leave the boy behind!"

V

The child was slumbering near the blaze:

    "O captain, let him rest

Until it sinks, when God's own ways

    Shall teach us what is best!"

The Song of the Wreck

They watch'd the whiten'd, ashy heap,

They touch'd the child in vain;

They did not leave him there asleep,

He never woke again.

Prologue to Wilkie Collins's Play

"The Frozen Deep"

1856

The Frozen Deep

THE second drama written by Wilkie Collins for the Tavistock House Theatre was first acted there in January, 1857, and subsequently at the Gallery of Illustration in the presence of Queen Victoria and the royal family. As in the case of "The Lighthouse," the play had the advantage of a Prologue in rhyme by Charles Dickens, who again electrified his audiences by marvellous acting, the character of Richard Wardour (a young naval officer) being selected by him for representation.

The Prologue was recited at Tavistock House

by John Forster, and at the public performances of the play by Dickens himself.

It is not generally known that a by no means inconsiderable portion of the drama was composed by Dickens, as testified by the original manuscripts of the play and of the prompt-book, which contain numerous additions and corrections in his handwriting. These manuscripts, by - the - way, realized three hundred pounds at Sotheby's in 1890.

The main idea of *A Tale of Two Cities* was conceived by Dickens when performing in "The Frozen Deep." "A strong desire was upon me then," he writes in the preface to the story, "to embody it in my own person; and I traced out in my fancy the state of mind of which it would necessitate the presentation to an

194

observant spectator, with particular care and interest. As the idea became familiar to me, it gradually shaped itself into its present form. Throughout its execution it has had complete possession of me: I have so far verified what is done and suffered in these pages, as that I have certainly done and suffered it all myself."

Prologue to
"The Frozen Deep"

(Curtain rises; mists and darkness; soft music throughout.)

ONE savage footprint on the lonely shore

Where one man listen'd to the surge's roar,

Not all the winds that stir the mighty sea

Can ever ruffle in the memory.

If such its interest and thrall, oh, then

Pause on the footprints of heroic men,

Making a garden of the desert wide

Where Parry conquer'd death and Franklin
  died.

To that white region where the lost lie low,

Wrapt in their mantles of eternal snow—

Unvisited by change, nothing to mock

Those statues sculptured in the icy rock,

We pray your company; that hearts as true

(Though nothings of the air) may live for
  you;

The Frozen Deep

Nor only yet that on our little glass

A faint reflection of those wilds may pass,

But that the secrets of the vast Profound

Within us, an exploring hand may sound,

Testing the region of the ice-bound soul,

Seeking the passage at its northern pole,

Softening the horrors of its wintry sleep,

Melting the surface of that "Frozen Deep."

Vanish, ye mists! But ere this gloom departs,

And to the union of three sister arts

We give a winter evening, good to know

That in the charms of such another show,

That in the fiction of a friendly play,

The Arctic sailors, too, put gloom away,

Forgot their long night, saw no starry dome,

Hail'd the warm sun, and were again at Home.

Vanish, ye mists! Not yet do we repair

To the still country of the piercing air;

But seek, before we cross the troubled seas,

An English hearth and Devon's waving trees.

A Child's Hymn

From "The Wreck of the Golden Mary"

1856

A Child's Hymn

THE Christmas number of *Household Words*
for 1856 is especially noteworthy as containing
the Hymn of five verses which Dickens con-
tributed to the second chapter. This made
a highly favorable impression, and a certain
clergyman, the Rev. R. H. Davies, was induced
to express to the editor of *Household Words*
his gratitude to the author of these lines for
having thus conveyed to innumerable readers
such true religious sentiments. In acknowl-
edging the receipt of the letter, Dickens ob-
served that such a mark of approval was none
the less gratifying to him because he was him-

self the author of the Hymn. "There cannot be many men, I believe," he added, "who have a more humble veneration for the New Testament, or a more profound conviction of its all-sufficiency, than I have. If I am ever (as you tell me I am) mistaken on this subject, it is because I discountenance all obtrusive professions of and tradings in religion, as one of the main causes why real Christianity has been retarded in this world; and because my observation of life induces me to hold in unspeakable dread and horror those unseemly squabbles about the letter which drive the spirit out of hundreds of thousands." — *Vide* Forster's *Life of Charles Dickens*, book xi. iii.

A Child's Hymn

HEAR my prayer, O heavenly
Father,

Ere I lay me down to sleep;

Bid Thy angels, pure and holy,

Round my bed their vigil keep.

My sins are heavy, but Thy mercy

Far outweighs them, every one;

Down before Thy cross I cast them,

Trusting in Thy help alone.

205

Keep me through this night of peril

Underneath its boundless shade;

Take me to Thy rest, I pray Thee,

When my pilgrimage is made.

None shall measure out Thy patience

By the span of human thought;

None shall bound the tender mercies

Which Thy Holy Son has bought.

Pardon all my past transgressions,

Give me strength for days to come;

Guide and guard me with Thy blessing

Till Thy angels bid me home.

THE END

Printed in the USA
CPSIA information can be obtained
at www.ICGtesting.com
LVHW020616150124
768656LV00006BB/450